Cryptocurrency:

How to Make a Lot of Money Investing and Trading in Cryptocurrency

Andrew Johnson

© **2017**

This declaration is deemed fair and valid by both the American Bar Association and the Committee of Publishers Association and is legally binding throughout the United States.

Furthermore, the transmission, duplication or reproduction of any of the following work, including precise information, will be considered an illegal act, irrespective whether it is done electronically or in print. The legality extends to creating a secondary or tertiary copy of the work or a recorded copy and is only allowed with express written consent of the Publisher. All additional rights are reserved.

The information in the following pages is broadly considered to be a truthful and accurate account of facts, and as such any inattention, use or misuse of the information in question by the reader will render any resulting actions solely under their purview. There are no scenarios in which the publisher or the original author of this work can be in any fashion deemed liable for any hardship or damages that may befall them after undertaking information described herein.

Additionally, the information found on the following pages is intended for informational purposes only and should thus be considered, universal. As befitting its nature, the information presented is without assurance regarding its continued validity or interim quality. Trademarks that mentioned are done without written consent and can in no way be considered an endorsement from the trademark holder.

DESCRIPTION

If you had purchased $100 worth of Bitcoins in the middle of 2009 then you would have ended up with 2,000 of them and really only been able to use them to buy drugs on the darknet. If you had held onto those coins until August 2017, you would have turned that $100 into more than $8,000,000. While the Bitcoin ship might have already sailed, it is not too late to jump onto the cryptocurrency bandwagon and make a profit in the process. If you are wondering about how to go about doing just that then *Cryptocurrency: How to Make a Lot of Money Investing and Trading in*

Cryptocurrency is the book you have been waiting for.

Currently, only about 25 percent of Americans actually understand what cryptocurrency is and only about 2 percent use them on a regular basis. Despite this fact, all of the more than 1,000 cryptocurrencies on the market today have a market valuation of more than $60 billion dollars. Regardless of what you know about cryptocurrency as a whole, it is clear that this market is something to watch. Inside you will learn everything you ever wanted to know about the technology that powers cryptocurrency and how to tell a Bitcoin from a Litecoin, from an Ether and why that distinction matters. You will also learn how to choose the most promising contenders for the Next Big Thing and not lose your shirt while taking advantage of the high degree of volatility that the market is currently experiencing.

Top analysts are already calling cryptocurrency the most important technological advancement since the internet and before the market settles down fortunes will most assuredly be won and lost several times over. So, what are you waiting for? Don't let this unique moment in human history pass you by, take control of your finances and buy this book today!

Inside you will find

- An easy to understand breakdown of blockchain, the foundational technology at the heart of all major cryptocurrencies.
- A detailed explanation of how cryptocurrencies lose and gain value and how you can put these methods to work for you.
- Easy ways to get started investing in cryptocurrencies and everything you will need in order to do so effectively.
- Recommendations on the major cryptocurrencies to watch moving forward.
- A step by step guide to getting started mining cryptocurrencies and making money off of other people's transactions.
- The best tips for staying one step ahead of the scammers out there who

are looking to steal your hard-earned cryptocurrency

- A look to the future including how major governments are looking to take control of cryptocurrency for their own ends.
- *And more...*

TABLE OF CONTENTS

INTRODUCTION

Congratulations on downloading *Cryptocurrency: How to Make a Lot of Money Investing and Trading in Cryptocurrency* and thank you for doing so. Cryptocurrency is an increasingly relevant investment concern and, even if you only have a vague idea of what it is all about at the moment, with a little bit of study you will soon find that there is significant profit to be made in that arena.

That doesn't mean that profit will be easy to acquire, however, which is why the following chapters will discuss everything you need to know in order to start investing in cryptocurrency in the most effective and reliable way possible. First, you will learn all about blockchain, the foundational technology in play behind all of the major cryptocurrencies currently on the market and just what it is about this technology that is causing experts to say it is the most important technological advancement since the creation of the internet. Next, you will learn all about the details of cryptocurrency itself and why you are sure to hear more about them in the immediate future.

From there, you will learn all about the ins and outs of investing in cryptocurrency in such a way that minimizes risk as much as possible while at the same time maximizing your potential for profit. You will then learn about tips for investing in cryptocurrency successfully along with avoiding fraud while doing so. You will also learn about the other major way to make money via cryptocurrency which is known as cryptocurrency mining. Finally, you will learn about when cryptocurrency is likely to go in the future.

There are plenty of books on this subject on the market, thanks again for choosing this one! Every effort was made to ensure it is full of as much useful information as possible, please enjoy!

CHAPTER 1:

UNDERSTANDING BLOCKCHAIN THE BUILDING BLOCK OF CRYPTOCURRENCY

Cryptocurrencies of one type or another are all the rage these days, despite the fact that approximately 75 percent of all Americans can't actually describe what a cryptocurrency is. Cryptocurrencies are a type of digital currency that can be put to use in an increasing number of ways from paying for groceries to making long-term investments. Their use and even their very existence came about thanks to the technology known as blockchain.

While the use of the term blockchain can vary depending on if the conversation in question is discussing cryptocurrency in general, smart contracts or Bitcoins, the main takeaway from the conversation is going to be that blockchain technology allows for the storage of large amounts of mostly financial data in a decentralized database. You may find it helpful to think of blockchain as you would Lego in that each blockchain is made up of a wide variety of blocks that can be assembled in different ways while still falling under the same general brand. More specifically, each blockchain stores data in such a way that it allows for an unparalleled combination of accessibility and security that is extremely difficult to crack due to its very nature.

Each block in a given blockchain contains all of the data from the preceding blocks while also adding its own unique information to the mix. Each time a new block is added to a chain from an established node, that information is then automatically added to all of the other nodes that are connected to that chain after it has been verified for accuracy. In addition to storing a vast swath of data, every block also automatically timestamps the transactions and it adds to the chain along with including other types of identifying data as well which makes it easy for the blockchain to determine its unique spot in the line of blocks.

This fact makes it easy for every blockchain to operate without any centralized control or authority directing it or any primary server that oversees the process to make sure everything works the way it should. Instead, these types of processes all take place automatically spread throughout the various nodes that are connected directly to the blockchain in question. As such, a single blockchain could easily be spread out across the entire world, based on nodes that are all operating more or less autonomously. These nodes then have the ability to communicate with one another securely through an advanced system that utilizes a form of specifically designed cryptography along with digital signals that are in place to ensure the integrity of the chain at all times.

Each blockchain allows for both read-only and writeable access depending on the authorization level of its users. Users that have read-only access are able to view the chain and its related transactions while writable users are allowed to add new blocks to the chain. Blockchain security is unique in that it doesn't work to actively prevent corruption from reaching the chain, instead, it relies on its unique nature to thwart those who have nefarious plans for the data encoded within. Altering the data contained within a blockchain would require extreme computational power that is not generally feasible or economical proposition for reasons that are outlined in detail below.

Innocuous beginnings

The root of blockchain technology can be traced all the way back to the 1980s when it was invented as a way to prevent spammers from sending out mass emails. The idea was that in order to send an email, the sender's computer would have to complete a basic calculation that would become increasingly more complex the more emails that are sent at once.

This technology never saw widespread use, and more or less lay fallow until 2008. At this point, discussion on a peer-to-peer programming forum turned to the ways at which the technology could be used as a way to facilitate P2P financial transactions that had no ties to the traditional banking infrastructure. This was a purely theoretical conversation at the time, but it didn't remain that way for long.

At the start of 2009, a treatise titled *Bitcoin: A P2P electronic cash system* started making the rounds on that same forum authored by a person or group of people using the pseudonym Satoshi Nakamoto. At about the same time this alias released the basic code of what would go on to form the basis of what would become the Bitcoin infrastructure, releasing the first round of Bitcoins as a proof of concept. A number of other programmers quickly went on to improve the code and the Nakamoto alias dropped off the map in early 2010.

To more accurately understand blockchain, it is helpful to understand how Bitcoin and a majority of the other cryptocurrencies on the market today actually work. Bitcoin is a type of digital currency that, in general, works the same way that other digital services such as PayPal do, though there are a few notable differences as well. It allows users to transfer Bitcoins from person to person with each

Bitcoin having a value that allows it to be exchanged for hard currency depending on its currently agreed upon value.

Each of these transactions is then recorded and verified in the Bitcoin blockchain which can then be viewed by anyone with the right software and a mind to do so. Each transaction is verified by individuals, referred to as Bitcoin miners, through the use of specialized hardware which completes the proof of work equation required to ensure that the transaction is authentic before new blocks are created. The miners are then paid for their time and electricity usage in fractions of Bitcoins for each transaction that they verify.

Bitcoins gain their value based on a global exchange rate at a given point in time-based, in part, on how many Bitcoins are currently on the market. Between July 2017 and August 2017, the price of Bitcoin has jumped more than $1,000 to sit at nearly $4,500. For reference, when the Nakamoto alias created the genesis block for the Bitcoin platform and released the first round of Bitcoins, one user then used 10,000 Bitcoins to order a pair of large pizzas which put the initial value of a Bitcoin at about $.002.

By 2014, Bitcoin, on the back of the blockchain technology that powered it, was catching on in the mainstream. When Bitcoin hit $1,000 in value for the first time, coders working on its infrastructure made a game-changing breakthrough. They discovered an easy way to add entire programs to individual blocks, creating the first smart contracts. The cryptocurrency Ethereum, discussed in detail later on in this book, has taken the smart contract concept and run with it, creating an entire platform based around this aspect of the blockchain technology.

Component of a blockchain

Decentralized database: The biggest difference between a traditional database and a blockchain database lies in the degree of centralization that is required for the database to function properly. In a standard

 database, data nodes and the servers that run them are split up based on physical space limitations but still kept as close to one another as possible as a means of reducing latency. On the other hand, decentralized databases, such as those used in the blockchain database are made up of nodes that have no physical limitations which means they can be spread out as much as the needs of their users require. This fact, when combined with blockchain's ability to self-sort components and its inherent tamper proof nature, means that it is largely autonomous in addition to being extremely safe. Blockchain more or less allows the

currency to move in the same way that the internet transfers information

Security measures: Perhaps the unique thing about blockchain technology is the security measures inherent in its cryptography. This security is a function of its decentralized nature in addition to being required because of it. It works based on the fact that each block contains all the information from the blocks that came before it. In order for a new block to be added to the chain, all of its information needs to be verified by nodes that are currently active around the world by comparing all of its information to that which came before it.

Unless the information in the new block matches the data that is stored in at least 51 percent of all active nodes, the new block will not be added to the existing blockchain. This means that in order for someone with malicious intent to submit a block with false information, they would need to coordinate a scenario where enough false nodes were created that they totaled more than half of all the nodes running the blockchain at one time.

Data: There are two types of data stored in each block of the blockchain, the data related to the block itself and the data containing all of its transactions. The data related to relevant transactions takes up most of the space and once it is verified it moves throughout all of the nodes of the blockchain through a process known as the best effort-model. This model allows information to be transferred to the closest nodes first, before spreading outward from node to node without the need for any controlling force.

Proof of work: Every time a new round of transactions is added to a node, that node is then verified against the blockchain's official timeline before being added to its place in the chain. Once this has taken place, the chain will then automatically log the relevant data and verify its proof of work system as a means of ensuring that the block was created via authorized means as opposed to outside forces. This proof of work requires a large amount of computational power in order to be completed successfully which is why miners are required and why they use specialized machines for the process. The more information a block requires, the more complicated its proof of work will be in order for it to be verified. This is another reason why it is so difficult and costly to hack a blockchain.

Hashes: Another facet of blockchain's security revolves around what are known as hashes, which ensure that even if someone broke into a blockchain they wouldn't be able to take advantage of what they saw and would instead see what is known as a fixed length output which is similar to a digital fingerprint. Changing so such as a single digit of a hash code then alters the data in ways that are impossible to predict. The most commonly used type of hash function that is used by a majority of available cryptocurrencies is what is known as SHA-256. The end result is that the data provided in this format can only be decoded by programs using the same program to decode it and make sure it is usable in a more traditional sense.

When a block is verified, it receives its own hash coded prior to being added to the chain. Each individual transaction is also given its own unique has as well. This starter hash is then modified even further based on the details relating to a block's specific location in the chain and the relation its data has to the blocks surrounding it. If the details of a block's hash don't match what they should when it reaches a new node the block will be removed from the chain.

Merkle trees: Merkle trees are a key part of not only how details are stored in the blockchain but also how they are accessed and verified relatively quickly. While blockchains can be built without them, those that don't take advantage of this technology are more difficult to access and tend to be less effective overall. As previously noted, each block contains numerous new transactions and each of these have their own hash code. The transactional hashes are then combined and put through an additional hacking process as they are added to the blockchain which causes another unique hash to be created as a result.

These hashes then continue to combine and multiply, getting larger and larger as they go until a single unique hash represents the blockchain as a whole. This fully completed hash is referred to as a root hash when is then used to the benefit of the Merkle tree, sometimes known as the Merkle chain. This chain can be thought of as the sum total of all the various hashes that are a part of it. The Merkle tree is then used as a means of additional security and also allows for the system to accurately determine when any of the hashes are altered. Each hash is then checked for accuracy each time an additional node is added to the chain.

Merkle trees are essentially what is known as a functionality matrix that allows each node to verify the current chain as effectively as possible. They also allow finances to be compacted into easily digested information that makes it easier for users to follow the flow of an individual transaction without needing to dig too deeply into all of the specifics.

Each Merkle tree starts with a pair of branches that split off into factors of two. These branches then also split and so on and so forth, allowing for an even distribution of data verification. They are also useful when it comes to encoding a variety of file types that are smaller than the original file. Merkle trees handle data verification in a fashion that is crucial to ensuring that a blockchain functions properly by allowing for the same information to exist in multiple places at the same time without having to worry about running the risk of corruption of accurate data just because some negligent data reaches the blockchain. This is what allows for the fact that data needs to be changed across a majority of nodes before it will be accepted by the blockchain as a whole.

The sheer amount of data that is stored in a blockchain means that checking each new block manually would be an extremely time-consuming process which is another reason that Merkle trees come in handy. They also make it easier to limit the amount of information that needs to be shared across all the relevant nodes at any given time which allows for each node to locate and determine disparities as quickly as possible by determining what the correct information actually is.

Each time a hash makes a match, it is flagged before the next branch is checked as a means of ensuring that everything matches up in a way of deciding the extent of the deviated information. This entire process takes much less time than it would if all of the data had to be individually checked each time a new block is added to the chain. Rather than rechecking all of the information each time a new block is added to the whole, the hashes are simply verified and the Merkle tree moves onto the next block.

Merkle trees require trust in order to function properly. Specifically, users must trust in the viability and sanctity of the blockchain as a whole. Thus, when a user decides to generate a new node, they can have faith that the version of the blockchain they are downloading is going to be the most recent version of the chain and also the most accurate. Any nodes that are generated by untrustworthy sources can then be easily checked against the primary hash. After everything has been approved and the download verified, it can then continue as normal. If the information generated by multiple nodes is proven to be inaccurate, they are then thrown out and the chain reverts back to the last version that was correctly verified.

While Merkle trees are generally used as a means to check for deviations in data structures and nodes, they are also gaining popularity when it comes to verifying similarities in the database and serves as well. Every website that relies on having servers that act as quickly as possible could benefit from this technology as it would allow their users to access information and connect to servers in a way that is as hassle-free as possible. If the database is then tampered with the hashes will change and the Merkle tree process will take note of these changes and set things right relatively quickly. This then stops any potential threats from taking root on a site before any of the malicious changes are permanent.

CHAPTER 2:

CRYPTOCURRENCY BASICS

For thousands of years prior to the existence of society as we know it today, the currency was essentially anything that was on hand and readily available. Barter was the way of the world and trade occurred whenever two people could come to an agreement on an even exchange between pigs and chickens or what have you. Slowly but surely urbanization begin to occur and, as individuals started to have fewer cows and chickens on hand, currencies began to take their place and made it easier for folks from varying regions to trade with one another

 with ease. The eventual creation of the internet essentially destroyed any barriers between worldwide commerce as individuals could trade money for objects from one side of the globe to the other.

After this most recent expansion of scope, denizens of the internet decided that the time was ripe for a purely digital medium of exchange and thus, cryptocurrencies were born. A cryptocurrency is any digital currency that is based on computer code and relies exclusively on the market to determine how new units are created and what the value of the currency is, as opposed to relying on hard assets like more traditional currencies. As an alternative to these currencies, cryptocurrencies have proven to be surprisingly viable over the past decade. They offer value in a purely digital fashion when it comes to tracking and issuing currency, all within a purely digital space.

Cryptocurrencies offer an autonomous means of tracking and control their units of currency in a self-contained sphere of influence without the need for a traditional governing body in anyshape or form. Bitcoin is currently the most famous example of this phenomena though there are more than one thousand types of cryptocurrency currently floating around on the internet and the darknet. Each of these cryptocurrencies have unique strengths and weaknesses and it is generally only considered a matter of time before an upstart dethrones Bitcoin as the modern face of cryptocurrencies. This is practically a given as each new cryptocurrency that comes into existence is built upon Bitcoin's strengths with steps taken to minimize their weaknesses.

Current contenders to watch include ether, the Ethereum currency which is primarily used as a way of paying for digital services and fueling digital machines which work on the back of smart contracts. The other major contender is Litecoin which offers confirmation times that are much faster than

Bitcoin's when it comes to verifying transactions.

While more standard currencies are limited based on external values when it comes to how much they could be worth, cryptocurrencies run the gauntlet from 1 cent all the way up to Bitcoin's $4,000+ valuation. There are two main forms of cryptocurrency, those that are controlled via a centralized source and those, such as Bitcoin that are at the complete and total whim of the market. Decentralized cryptocurrencies such as Bitcoin tend to utilize a wide variety of different verification methods when it comes to making sure that transactions get to where they need to be and are verified and added to the appropriate blockchain in the process. This is commonly done through the proof-of-work model though there are other viable options such as consensus platforms and consensus protocols as well.

How cryptocurrency is priced

As there are no governing bodies watching over cryptocurrency prices, it falls to each cryptocurrency to maintain its price using different means. The price of a particular cryptocurrency is a reflection of the value that the market assigns to it, which means that at its core it is still a reflection of supply and demand, though arguably in a purer form than more traditional currencies. External factors are also known to play a bigger role in cryptocurrencies than with traditional currencies purely because there are fewer filters between them and the market forces that drive them.

Those who spend their type trading in cryptocurrencies generally have a measurable role in the determination of price, especially among cryptocurrencies that are less well-known to the general public, or at least the small percentage of the public that is aware of cryptocurrencies in the first place. These traders operate just like any other trader in that they purchase a given cryptocurrency, hold it until they can make a profit and then sell it off again to someone else who is interested in repeating the process. If enough traders purchase and hold onto a given cryptocurrency then they can conspire to inflate the price to levels that are higher than what demand would otherwise dictate.

While it is sometimes positive, if you happen to be holding onto the currency, outside influences can also often be negative, driving the price of a specific cryptocurrency down regardless of what market demand might otherwise dictate. If this occurs, the creators of the currency have frequently been seen to step in the past and attempt to use other external forces as a means of cutting off these downward trends. Some of the ways they do so are discussed here:

Coverage in the media: Regardless of the type of media that is used, coverage in the media is one of the primary means by which the price of a given cryptocurrency is manipulated by outside forces as it gives those who are only aware of cryptocurrency in a general sense something to focus all of their energy on. This artificially generated public interest then leads to an increase in price as investors rush to jump onto the next big thing. The media often perks up when a new cryptocurrency begins showing up on the major cryptocurrency exchanges or if an option that has already previously been mentioned receives a major update to its code. Additional media worthy events include facts that can be succinctly summed up by sound bites or anything that proves it is a market that is growing in community involvement and overall popularity. Regardless of the context, media coverage is likely to increase the price of the cryptocurrency that receives the coverage.

General opinions: The internet is naturally divided into subgroups that are all intensely devoted to a specific thing. This goes for every type of cryptocurrency, no matter how obscure it is to the wider world and these individuals can be thought of as the cryptocurrency's vanguard when it comes to convincing the wider world that they are using a viable platform. These subgroups can be a powerful force when it comes to artificially inflating the price of their chosen cryptocurrencybecause the more they can get their message out there, the more likely it will be that other people will bite and invest money into it. Furthermore, these vanguards also provide valuable feedback to developers, work on the code that supports the cryptocurrencythemselves and invest their own money into it, each of which helps drive the price higher.

The clearest example of this type of scenario occurred during the initial Bitcoin bubble in 2014. At this point, Bitcoin had slowly been growing in value for about five years before suddenly hitting a tipping point in its user base. Once this occurred the price of something that had previously been worth less than a dollar rapidly increased until the price was greater than $1,000. As a result of this increase, serious investors started taking notice for the first time and the price has largely been on a positive trajectory ever since.

Automated bots: Just like with any other currency, liquidity is a crucial part of a cryptocurrency's growth, after all, if there isn't any available currency to trade, the public interest will drop off and the price will dip as a result. Unlike with hard currencies, if a specific cryptocurrency isn't growing at a rate that its creators appreciate, they can deploy bots to get in on the trading action and artificially inflating the amount of liquidity available, thus ensuring things continue moving in the desired direction. Liquidity relates to the amount of a given asset that is currently available to trade and if it is low then those looking to trade in a specific cryptocurrency won't have any means of purchasing it.

To counter this fact, automated bots are employed as a means to sell and buy the targeted cryptocurrency, stimulating growth through what are an essentially simulated transaction which often causes additional units of the currency to be produced in response, thus improving liquidity overall. This is particularly prevalent in China which has far fewer restrictions on cryptocurrency exchanges than the rest of the world. In fact, they are regularly credited with creating a large amount of the liquidity that Bitcoin takes advantage of on a regular basis.

Social media presence: When it comes to traditional currencies, relevant news tends to spread through traditional means such as newspapers and targeted television programs. With cryptocurrency, however, relevant news and policy changes are far more likely to first come to light via social media. There are countless groups across all social media platforms that are dedicated to cryptocurrency trading and those who follow it religiously and these followers are typically rabid for their chosen cause. This level of enthusiasm means that it will only take a small mention of a change to a given cryptocurrency, even if it is unverified, to cause enough movement in that cryptocurrency to affect the market.

This fact has generated a unique phenomenon where those with a financial interest in a particular cryptocurrency can easily spread blatantly false rumors about it as a way to make prices move in the direction they prefer, even past the point where the rumor in question is proven to be without merit. If this rumor was directly related to a price increase or decrease then it often comes true simply based on public reaction and completely without taking into account what the market would have actually done otherwise.

Pump and dump: This is a type of influencing that has been going on with traditional currencies for generations and has, unsurprisingly, made its way into the cryptocurrency markets where it is frowned upon but not against the law. The pump and dump works when an individual or group of individuals purchases up as much of a given cryptocurrency as possible, thus limiting the amount available to the public at large, driving up the price as a result of the perceived shortage.

Cryptocurrency exchanges operate via what are known as digital order books which create lists of all of the cryptocurrency trades made each day. If those books end up being light on sellers and heavy on buyers, the price changes as a result. After the price has increased in proportion to the amount of scarcity that has been created, those who initiated the pump and dump sell off all of the cryptocurrency that they purchased, achieving a significant windfall in the process. This part of the process then sends the price into the dumpster as the demand will suddenly dramatically decrease when compared to the supply.

Common cryptocurrency considerations

While Bitcoin is without a doubt the most commonly discussed cryptocurrency these days, it is a long way from the only game in town. The following list outlines the details of several different cryptocurrencies that are also worth keeping an eye on. Keep in mind that this is only a brief overview, however, the specifics described here are always in flux and new and it is impossible to say when a new potentially game-changing cryptocurrency may appear on the market. All of the cryptocurrencies discussed here can be purchased on any reputable cryptocurrency exchange.

Ether: The biggest contender for the crown these days is the Ethereum currency known as ether. Ether is mostly used between individuals to fund services, primarily those that are based on smart contracts. It is also used to provide what is known as gas for virtual machines that have become something of an Ethereum hallmark. This gas covers the operating costs of the individual systems as well as the system as a whole. Approximately 18 million ether is created each year.

Ether is especially worth keeping an eye on, as by the end of 2017 it will switch from a proof-of-work validation to what is known as a proof-of-stake validation system. This means instead of assigning validation services to a random assortment of miners, those with a stake in the transaction in question will have the opportunity to verify the transaction. Blocks will then be forged instead of mined and foragers will receive transaction fees for their work but will not be paid an additional stipend in the traditional sense.

Furthermore, in early 2017, numerous research groups, along with Fortune 500 companies an various blockchain startup companies all got together (more than one hundred in all) to form the nonprofit organization known as the Ethereum Alliance whose purpose is to create a standard for the open-source version of the Ethereum blockchain along with a private version that will specifically address the needs of professional industries including healthcare and banking in a more focused way.

With the Ethereum blockchain, smart contracts are store on every node in a public fashion which means it can sometimes be difficult for nodes to calculate so much data, with the end result being lower verification speeds. The Ethereum is currently capable of processing approximately 25 transactions each second, though great scalability is said to be possible. As of July 2017, one ether is worth approximately $200.

Litecoin: Litecoin is the cryptocurrency that currently bears the greatest similarity to Bitcoin, but with a few important improvements thrown in for good measure. It can process far more transaction in a shorter period of time than Bitcoin can which prevents many of the bottlenecks that the Bitcoin network frequently experiences. In fact, it can process approximately five times as many blocks as blockchain in the same period of time. The downside is its methods tend to lead to more orphan blocks but at the same time, it has less chance of leading to a double-spending scenario where the same coins are spent twice while the nodes catch up.

Furthermore, it also requires significantly less processing power to verify a Litecoin than it does a Bitcoin. It also offers very low payments costs and completes payments approximately four times faster than Bitcoin does. The Litecoin network is working to produce as many as 84 million Litecoins which dwarfs the number of Bitcoins on the market nearly 4 to 1. In July 2017, 1 Litecoin was worth approximately $42.

Dogecoin: While first introduced as a joke on the concept of cryptocurrency, which is why its logo features a picture of the Shiba Inu dog made popular by the 2013 meme, it has since gone on to be one of the most high-profile forms of cryptocurrency outside of

Bitcoin. In fact, a crowdfunding campaign was successfully funded to send a solid gold dogecoin to the moon in 2019. In its first month of existence in 2013, it reached a capitalization of over $60 million. It is also different than many other cryptocurrencies as it has a production schedule of 5.26 billion coins produced per year. It is most commonly used as a way for social media users to tip one another on particularly interesting posts.

Dogecoin also offers a very fast one-minute processing time and has no limit on the number that can ultimately be generated. It was worth approximately $1250 in July of 2017.

CHAPTER 3: GETTING STARTED INVESTING IN CRYPTOCURRENCY

2016 saw a dramatic growth in the capitalization of cryptocurrencies of all shapes and sizes which makes them attractive to a wide swath of the investment market. Once again, Bitcoin remains the reigning champ, both as the most stable cryptocurrency on the market and the one that showed the greatest overall increase in 2016 at 300 percent. This doesn't mean that investing in cryptocurrencies is without risk, however, which is why it is important to keep in mind the pros and cons outlined below before making any serious investments into this rapidly changing market.

Benefits

Decreased chance of fraud: Due to the fact that cryptocurrencies are all-digital it makes it much more difficult for traditional types of fraud to occur around them. They cannot be counterfeited, or forged, and it is impossible for one person in the transaction to sneakily reverse it once it has gone through.

Protection against identity theft: After you have purchased a cryptocurrency you don't need to worry about identity theft the way you do when you are dealing with more traditional exchanges. This is a serious concern when it comes to typical exchanges as each new transaction brings along additional charges to your debit or credit card which, in turn, means that there are always new opportunities for thieves to do something nefarious.

Extreme access: Currently, there are three billion people in the world who have access to the internet but do not have regular access to any form of exchange. This leaves the cryptocurrency market with a lot of room to maneuver and it is expected to see significant growth as it gains wider acceptance. This means that an increasing amount of business is going to take place purely through digital currencies which means those who invest in cryptocurrency now aren't just likely to see an increase, they are likely to see a dramatic increase. For example, as of 2017, fifty percent of all Kenyans now own a Bitcoin wallet while less than forty percent have access to reliably clean water and only thirty percent have modern plumbing.

Less cost: Despite the fact that every cryptocurrency transaction comes with an accompanying transaction fee, the fees for utilizing a cryptocurrency exchange are almost always going to be lower than what the traders who use more traditional exchanges pay on a regular basis.

Negatives

Future is uncertain: Despite the fact that Bitcoin has proved to be a winning investment for at least three years, cryptocurrency markets as a whole are still extremely new and all the risks associated with them are extremely ill-defined when compared to traditional markets. This means that, while profits are currently quite frequently higher than other markets, there are no guarantees that these trends will persist or when the bottom might fall out on the market. There simply isn't the data required to determine where they are likely to be in six months, much less a year or five years from now which means the potential for loss is essentially limitless. Until the market stabilizes in the long-term there is no way of telling if each dollar you put into the cryptocurrency market will be worth more next year than it is today.

High volatility: Despite the fact that Bitcoin is the most stable of all the 1,000+ cryptocurrencies, it is still more than five times as volatile as gold and more than six times as volatile as the S&P 5000. While volatility means a greater chance at profit, it also means that the chance that a catastrophic loss might wipe out the market is very real. Additionally, roughly 80 percent of all cryptocurrencytransactions are speculative as of 2017 with buyers simply buying it up and waiting for a price increase which means the bubble has to burst eventually.

Purely digital: While cryptocurrency's digital nature is widely seen as one of its biggest benefits, the fact that there isn't anything in the real world backing it up means it has its downsides as well. All of the details regarding every cryptocurrency exchange on the planet only exists on hard drives and modern hard drives which are in no ways infallible. If the exchange you decide to utilize experience technical issues then there is no way to be sure that your investment might not simply disappear leaving you with few options when it comes to recouping funds.

The sheer potential for profits if a hacker does manage to break into an exchange means they are constantly looking for security weaknesses to exploit which means they are occasionally going to be successful. As an example, Ethereum has seen numerous attacks over the years, one of which was so successful that an entirely new chain had to be constructed in order to repair the damage. Those that chose not to migrate their accounts are now trading on Ethereum Classic. Splits like this would literally never happen in the real world and goes to show just how unpredictable things can get if you choose to trade in uncharted waters.

Cryptocurrency trading

Trading cryptocurrencies can be an extremely profitable investment approach, regardless of how familiar you are with the ins and outs of securities trading. One of the best things about trading in cryptocurrency is that there is practically no barrier to entry. To get started, all you need to do is find an exchange that seems legitimate based on a reasonable amount of research and then go ahead and make your first trade. If you are already the proud owner of an amount of cryptocurrency you are hoping to trade then in many cases your account won't even need to be verified.

Another great thing about trading in cryptocurrency is that the market is frequently extremely fragmented which leads to large spreads than you would generally see anywhere else. Due to the fact that cryptocurrency exchanges are not officially regulated by anyone, they also offer the ability to trade with extremely large margins in place which means a small investment can become a large return there practically faster than anywhere else, the same goes for losses, however, so caution is suggested. To add in another layer of complexity, no two exchanges are connected which means each is free to change prices based on their own levels of supply and demand. This, in turn, leads to opportunities for arbitrage as you can often pick up a currency on one exchange and sell it on another, immediately, and still turn a profit.

Furthermore, due to the fact that Bitcoin is still considered the cryptocurrency standard, many of the cryptocurrencies on the market have followed its lead when it comes to creating and sustaining price bubbles which are supported by outside influences as discussed in the previous chapter. While this won't be good for those who waited until the bubble was in place to buy in, those who got in before the current boom cycle will stand to make a pretty penny as long as they get out while the getting is good.

The most common means for trading cryptocurrencies through trading companies is via what is known as a contract for differences (CFD). With these types of contracts, a buyer and seller make an agreement and when the agreement expires, the buyers will pay the seller the difference in price from when the contract was agreed upon to the current moment, assuming things end up in a net gain. If the price decreases during that time then the seller owes the difference to the buyer instead.

As far as leverage is concerned, rates of as much as 20 to 1 are not uncommon which means that a $1 investment can net you $20 per each dollar the price increases, per unit that you purchased of the cryptocurrency in question. While this means the potential for making a profit is extremely robust, the potential for loss is equally strong which means you are going to want to be very aware of your odds of success before taking on any leveraged trades.

Additional benefits

Global currencies: Traditional currencies are fairly limited when it comes to external factors that affect their price. This is not the case with cryptocurrencies, however, as anything serious that happens anywhere in the world has the potential to impact price movement based on how investors respond to the news. As an example, Bitcoin has seen significant price movements based on everything from the implementation of new capital controls in Greece to the Chinese devaluing the Yuan. Events such as these have actually caused many of Bitcoin's largest swings in price throughout the years, both positive and negative.

The market never closes: Blowing even the forex market, which is open 120 hours per week, out of the water, the cryptocurrency markets are open 24/7, 365 days of the year. Additionally, there are currently more than 100 different cryptocurrency exchanges that see a large amount of usage and they all offer various levels of trading and different rates which means it shouldn't be hard to find the one that is right for you and your trading or investment goals.

These two factors also affect volatility as any event anywhere and at any time can cause an immediate response among cryptocurrency investors. Swings of greater than five percent in a single day are relatively common amongst the major cryptocurrencies and the smaller cryptocurrencies have been known to swing as much as fifteen percent in a single day.

Finding the right exchange

Prior to putting your money into a specific exchange, it is extremely important to do your homework as a means of preventing yourself from ending up in a position where your exchange of choice simply calls it a day and packs up shop, taking your money with them.

Remember, if this does occur you are unlikely to have any real recourse of any kind which means you are going to want to do your best to make a wise choice right from the beginning.

Consider transparency: One of the most important things you will need to consider is the level of transparency the exchange you are looking at operates under. You should be able to freely take a look at their order book in addition to general information about where their funds are kept and how they verify their reserve currency. If this type of information is not readily available, then the exchange simply might not have the means to do so, or it may be much worse than that. Exchanges that don't make their details public are often what is known as fractional exchanges which means that they do not keep enough cryptocurrency on hand to cover all of their debts which means they are likely to fold if there is ever a run on the cryptocurrency that they focus on as they will be unable to fulfill all the requests.

Security level: It is important to always take into account the level of security that your chosen exchange operates under. The bare minimum level of security required is a basic online security protocol which means that its URL will have an HTTPS in it rather than an HTTP. A secure protocol allows for a greatly decreased risk of a personal information leak which means there is less of a chance for your account to be stolen. Additionally, you are going to want to go above and beyond and ensure that the one you choose has a two-factor identification process as well as secure login practices. If you commit to an exchange with less than this then all you are doing is opening yourself up to the possibility of identity theft.

Be aware of fees

Regardless of the type of cryptocurrency you are buying into, you will need to pay a transaction fee to the person who verifies it for you. While, technically, most of these transaction fees are voluntary, if you elect not to pay them then cryptocurrency miners have a much less impressive incentive to taking and verifying your block which means you will have to wait longer for your money to appear if you do so. A majority of the changes in the world, outside of China, then charge a secondary fee on top of the transaction fee as a way for the exchange to turn a profit. These secondary fees can add up quickly if you aren't careful which is why it is important to know what's up before you commit to a specific exchange.

Local is better: While there are cryptocurrency exchanges all over the world, you are going to want to prioritize those in your own country for the best results. First and foremost, this will make it easier for you to take advantage of local periods of heavier trading simply because you are more likely to be awake when they occur. Furthermore, you are going to be more likely to be able to get the help that you can understand if something goes wrong and you need to contact customer support. Even better, depending on your country, and its regulations, you may even be able to accept some semblance of recourse should the worst happen and the exchange fold which means you will at least stand a chance of getting your money back. There is still no guarantee on this front, however, so be sure to read up on local regulations rather than blindly putting your faith in the system.

Additionally, it is important to keep in mind that just because you choose a local exchange doesn't necessarily mean they are going to be dealing in the currencies that you hope they might. USD is still the most common currency for these exchanges to deal in which means if you are looking for another primary currency you may need to look a little harder for an exchange that deals in it.

Know how long the transactions will take: Due to the fact that all cryptocurrency transactions require verification before they go through, exchange transactions tend to work on a lead time that gives this process time to occur. It is important that you take the time to read up on the amount of time that your chosen exchange takes to do such things in order to be aware of how long it will take to actually get the cryptocurrency of your choice before you pull the trigger. Regardless of the lag time, you are going to want to choose an exchange that locks in rates when the trade is initiated rather than when it goes through otherwise you will often find yourself potentially making less than you would have otherwise, simply due to the transaction time required. This will also ensure that you don't miss out on profitable trades because things were lagging.

Popular exchanges

Kraken: This exchange is one of the top 15 in the USD market in addition to being the most popular of the Euro-friendly exchanges. So much so that it clears more Euro volume than any other currently active cryptocurrency exchange.

Coinbase: This is the oldest continuously active cryptocurrency exchange currently active in the United States. It is closely regulated and is still in the top five when it comes to volume of cryptocurrency exchanged per day.

OKCoin: This is a Chinese exchange which means it is far less regulated than the other options on this list. The only reason it makes on the list at all is because it primarily deals in USD.

Bitstamp: This is another one of the oldest continuously operating cryptocurrency exchanges on the market today. It was first started in 2011 and is still the second most commonly used, exchanging more than 10,000 units of currency each and every day.

Bitfinex: This is the most popular exchange on the market today, with users all over the world trading nearly 200,000 units of currency each week. If you are already in possession of cryptocurrency then you can get started trading with Bitfinex without having to deal with any amount of external verification.

ICOs

Initial coin offerings (ICOs) are an increasingly common occurrence. In 2017 a new cryptocurrency known as Bancor managed to raise $153 million in a matter of hours and another known as Status.im raising nearly $70 million in that same period of time. Overall, in 2017 alone, this process has raised nearly half a billion dollars for a variety of cryptocurrencies.

While the name comes from the more commonly known initial public offering, ICOs are significantly different in nearly every way.

In general, an ICO is a type of crowdfunding strategy that businesses that are based on blockchain technology can implement as a means of funding their business plans. Investors are provided with the opportunity to buy into the cryptocurrency that the company is creating at a fixed rate before it hits the general market. These early investors are essentially betting that the resulting cryptocurrency or application that is being created is going to be popular enough to warrant a high enough demand to cause the currency to rise above whatever it is that they paid for it. Currently, the Ethereum platform has been the platform of choice for many of the most popular ICOs to date.

While much of this funding is coming in from China, investors from all over the world have been known to jump in on the ground floor of these ICOs, all the while hoping that they are going to catch on in a serious way. In addition to the standard warnings that go along with investing into an essentially unknown quantity, ICOs face unique issues that make them far from a reliable investment. Most importantly, there are concerns at the federal level that these companies are avoiding SEC regulations which means their business plans are not currently held up to the same rigorous standards as IPOs. Additionally, critics are claiming that the success they have seen so far is simply part of another bubble that has yet to burst, much like the Bitcoin bubble has done several times over the last eight years.

Despite these potential issues, ICOs still have the possibility to produce serious profits for early investors as they will most assuredly see a high-return on their investments if everything goes according to plan. Regardless, if you are thinking about pursuing this investment path then you will need to keep in mind that if investing in cryptocurrency in the standard way is risky, then investing in ICOs is downright dangerous. As will all investments, it is important that you never make the mistake of investing more than you can afford to lose.

As such, you are going to want to approach any ICO with an analytical mindset which means you are going to want to start by looking at any available documentation that the company will provide, including a business plan. This will allow you to make sure that the project makes financial sense at the base level and that its long-term business proposition checks out. You will also need to ensure that the market has already shown an actual demand for the product or service that the company is planning to provide. Additionally, you will want to make sure that the cryptocurrency that is being offered will end up being a vital part of the business that is being created when it is actually up and running.

It is also important to remember that buying into an ICO is not the same as buying stock through a standard IPO. When you buy into an IPO you are literally buying into a company, buying into an ICO gives you no such rights. What's more, IPOs come with certain requirements for the company in question including fiduciary and accreditation obligations from the company, ICOs have no such requirements.

With most ICOs, you will be lucky to see a website, a business plan and a white paper, and maybe not even all three of these. As they have never yet had a product ready to show off, you are risking a great deal more than with any other type of investment scenarios.

It is also important to note that just because these companies are seeing a strong response at first, doesn't mean this goodwill is going to last. What's more, many venture capitalists actually believe that giving a new company so much money up front is actually detrimental to the long-term health of the company as those in charge often feel compelled to spend what they have without feeling the need to work as hard as possible to create a product that people actually want.

Finally, the fact that a majority of these companies are creating products based on the Ethereum platform should be a cause for concern as well, simply because it is just another cryptocurrency platform, albeit one that those in the know believe has a better chance than most of making it in the long-term. This is still just conjecture, however, and there is nothing to prevent the Ethereum platform from experiencing a series of flash crashes and vanishing within six months. After all, it is still very much experimental, and thus immature, technology. All told, ICOs are a very risky, but potentially profitable venture which means it might be in your best interest to wait until some of the currently ICO companies actually pan out before getting involved in the process directly.

CHAPTER 4: INVESTING IN CRYPTOCURRENCY TIPS FOR SUCCESS

Understanding investment

Investing successfully is all about working smarter as opposed to harder. Rather than working long hours and sacrificing personal happiness to sock money away in a savings account, it is about taking that money and using it to potentially build a better life in the long run through a maximization of profits earn. Investing successfully is also about setting priorities for your money and the returns it will generate. Spending is easy to

 do and provides instant gratification and short-term satisfaction. On the other hand, investing is all about delayed gratification and making life better in the long-term.

Increased returns: One of the most important aspects of investing is what is known as compounding which is the process of generating larger returns in the long-term by reinvesting initial returns both early and often. In order for it to work out in your favor, it requires both time and initial earnings for you to reinvest. If given enough of both factors, compounding can help an initial investment grow exponentially over time. If you are lucky enough to still be 20 or more years away from retirement then compounding should be thought of as the most important investment tool in your arsenal.

For example, if you are currently 25 years old and want to save a million dollars by the time you are ready to retire at age 60, you would need to invest a little less than $900 per month, assuming you were going to maintain a steady five percent return on your investments for the next 35 years. On the other hand, if you wait to start investing until you are 35 then you will need to invest about twice as much to reach the same point. Finally, if you wait 20 years and don't start investing until you are 45, then you would need to save four times as much to reach your goal.

Know what type of investing suits you best: The reason that there are so many different investment strategies out there is that there is no strategy out there that is right for everyone. Each investor has different reasons for wanting to invest, different acceptable levels of risk, different metrics for success and a different desired timeframe.

First and foremost, it is important that you determine the goals you have for your overall investment strategy. For some people, this will be keeping their principal intact while others are going to be willing to risk it all in order to accumulate more in the long-term. Depending on your goals, you may even want to create different isolated investments to reach each of them. Regardless of what your plans are before you get started investing it is crucial that you have a clear idea in mind about why you are doing what you are doing as this will make it easier to determine the best way to actually getting results. You are also going to want to keep in mind that your goals will not be completed in a vacuum which means you will need to be aware of your overall timeframe as well as how much risk you are willing to take on in order to ensure that you end up with goals that are actually achievable as opposed to useless flights of fancy.

Prior to being able to accurately determine your goals, it is important to decide for yourself how much money you feel you would be alright with losing, as this will make it easier to determine your overall level of risk. When deciding on this amount it is important to keep in mind that no investment, regardless of how safe it may seem in the grand scheme of things is without risk and that it is this risk that ultimately leads to profit. The amount of risk you are going to be able to safely deal with is going to be, in part, about how quickly you hope to see a return on your initial investment. If you have 20 years or more of investing ahead of you then you will be able to safely take on additional risk when compared to someone who is just a few years away from retirement.

After you have determined your current level of risk aversion, you are also going to need to consider how much time you are going to want to spend micromanaging your investments. If you are looking for an investment strategy that allows you to spend relatively little time thinking about your investments then you are going to want to move forward with what is known as a buy-and-hold strategy where you would buy into one of the more stable types of cryptocurrencies, such as Bitcoin, and hold onto it for a prolonged period of time in order to see reliable, if not necessarily stellar, returns. If you are instead looking to spend a lot of time maximizing your potential returns then you will want to look into riskier ventures that have a greater chance of paying off big-time if you watch them carefully.

Next, you will need to consider how knowledgeable you are when it comes to the investments you are going to be making as well as how comfortable you are going to be when it comes to monitoring your investments and making decisions about their future. Your investment decisions should always be based on how much time you have to dedicate to research and your overall comfort level with the investment process. Remember, it is important to be up front with yourself when it comes to knowing what you don't know. Above all else, you are going to want to avoid being talked into investments that you have not thoroughly vetted yourself and never, no matter what, invest more than you can afford to lose regardless of how much of a sure thing the investment might appear to be on the surface.

Diversification is key: Regardless of how good a particular investment might seem up front, it is always a better idea to split your investment fund into at least two places as opposed to doubling down on just one investment. This is where creating a portfolio comes into play and it is an important part of investing in the long-term that everyone should consider regardless of their goals or experience. Diversifying will also help to protect your investments in case the cryptocurrency you are primarily interested in suddenly starts to experience serious loss. The way you should ultimately decide to distribute your money is going to be a result of your tolerance for risk, how comfortable you are with investing in general and how much time you are willing to commit to micromanaging your investments.

Know when to get out: If you are planning to invest in the long-term then inevitably your investments are going to end up taking a hit from time to time and, as such the value of your overall portfolio will dip. This is a natural part of the investment process and, in general, your best bet is going to be to stay the course and wait for things to turn back around. This is not always going to be the case, however, and any time your investments start to dip you will need to do some research and figure out exactly what happened. If the reason for the dip is more or less benign then there is no reason to sell as long as the investment has produced reliable results so far.

However, if your research reveals something larger that is taking place, then this initial loss may only be the tip of the iceberg, if this is the case then you will want to prepare yourself to move out of the investment in such a way that maximizes your potential for profit before you end up losing your shirt. It is important to approach your potential investments in such a way that emotion doesn't enter into the equation in any way shape or form. If your research indicates that additional losses are forthcoming, then it will not do you any good to hold onto the investment and wish that things will turn around. If you hope to see successful results from your investments in the long-term, getting attached to the investments you have made is simply not an option.

Cryptocurrency investment tips

While first getting started with investing in cryptocurrency is as easy as finding an exchange and making your first trade, investing successfully is another thing entirely. The following are a list of things you are going to need to keep in mind if you want to successfully invest in this burgeoning market in the long-term.

Treat cryptocurrency the way you would any other commodity: Commodities and cryptocurrencies are actually relatively similar from an investment standpoint for several reasons. First, is that they are both used for more than just investment purposes; commodities are real world assets such as base metals that are used in industrial projects, precious metals find use in the jewelry market, and cryptocurrencies are increasingly being used to power a wide variety of things thanks to smart contracts. Furthermore, both are traded through open market exchanges. As such, when it comes to choosing the right cryptocurrency to invest in, you are going to want to choose the one that appears as though it is going to add value to the real world and contains multiple probable uses outside of standard P2P transactions.

Usage is on the rise: When taken together as a whole, all the cryptocurrencies currently on the market have a combined cap of roughly

$60 billion. To put this into perspective, Coca Cola's market cap is about $180 billion, Boeing's is $100 billion and Tesla's is $50 billion. What makes this number meaningful, is that real-world usage has gone hand in hand with the increasing market usage which means it is unlikely that cryptocurrencies as a whole will be going away anytime soon, regardless of how anyone individual cryptocurrency might fair. As such, while the day-to-day market remains extremely volatile, as a long-term investment cryptocurrency is looking increasingly stalwart.

Additionally, despite the amount of buzz in investment circles about them, the number of people who use them regularly or are even aware of their existence is still an extremely small portion of the population as a whole. Currently, only about 2 percent of Americans use any type of cryptocurrency on a regular basis and on 25 percent can accurately define what a Bitcoin is. Compared to their market cap, this is an extremely encouraging number that has literally nowhere to go but up, taking prices with it.

These numbers are increasingly important as, regardless of which you plan on investing in, the more people who use them on a regular basis, the more profitable they are going to be for those who invest in them. Furthermore, a steady increase in users will eventually even out the issue they currently have with generating pricing bubbles which means the prices will be less likely to dramatically decrease at any point as well.

Market cycle: The market cycle is a way of looking at the pattern that all investments eventually follow sooner or later when looked at over a long enough timeline. The market cycle starts with optimism on the positive side, switches into thrill as it continues moving upward, peaks at euphoria and then begins to drop through anxiety, denial, fear, and depression before reaching its lowest level at panic. It then eventually begins to move upward again through depression, hope and relief before getting back to optimism.

While Bitcoin has already been through the entire cycle once, bottoming out during the 2014 crash, virtually every other cryptocurrency on the market is still in the optimism stage which means there is still plenty of time for those in the know to take advantage of it. If you do your investment research properly you could easily see up to five solid years of growth before any of them reach the euphoria stage which, coincidentally, is about how long experts anticipate it will take for cryptocurrency as a whole to reach market saturation.

While it is important to keep the state of the market in mind, it is also important to realize that, much like the dot-com boom of the 90s, approximately eighty percent of all the cryptocurrencies created between now and the point at which the market reaches the saturation point, will not survive into the saturation phase. This is simply a fact of the way the market works as they will simply not be able to survive throughout the buildup and hype that will cause many investors to throw their money at something without taking the time to assess whether or not that cryptocurrency actually does anything to increase the value of the market. Rather, they will simply focus on locating the best apparent deal and watching the price rise while more and more of their contemporaries make the same mistake.

Focus on solving problems: Regardless of how much profit a given cryptocurrency may potentially make, buying into it and sitting back to watch what happens is never going to be the most effective strategy possible. Rather, you are going to want to put in the extra time and energy to find those cryptocurrencies that legitimately solve problems that the world at large, or at least the market, is currently having a hard time coping with. The bigger the problem it solves, the more likely it is that it will be a viable long-term investment because the greater its overall value will eventually shake out to be.

As a major portion of the world at large does not have easy access to the type of reliable banking that some countries take for granted, this means that cryptocurrencies offer a reliable way to fill these needs. They can provide functions such as wiring money and easy payments between individuals and the cryptocurrencies that do this the best are going to be the ones that will survive past the saturation point.

Focus on the long-term: It is important that your cryptocurrency portfolio is focused exclusively on the long-term. It is also important that you vary your investments in such a way that you limit your overall risk as much as possible. Additionally, it is best to limit the overall amount of cryptocurrencies that you invest into somewhere between three and five. Above all else, it is important to make a concentrated effort to control your emotions and never make rash decisions when your investments are on the line.

You will also need to keep in mind that unlike with many types of long-term investment, investing in cryptocurrency brings with it no lock-in risk as they can be exchanged or other types of currency whenever you deem fit rather than being committed to only being traded. This means that investing in cryptocurrency is really no different than storing cash except that the potential for a return on your investment is much higher than with a traditional savings account.

Be aware of Ethereum

While Bitcoin is still the king, at $4,000 per Bitcoin it isn't really the up and coming type of investment you should be focusing on in hopes of returning a maximum profit. This honor currently goes to the Ethereum platform and its currency, ether. The number of transactions on the Ethereum blockchain is about half of what Bitcoin has completed to date, despite the fact that it has been around for only a third of the time of its primary competitor.

What's even more important is that unlike the transaction chart for Bitcoin which is riddled with steep declines in price, the Ethereum chart is much more bullish overall as of summer 2017. Cryptocurrencies are inherently social constructs which means they have robust network effects which means that as the adoption of Ethereum continues to increase its value and utility will do the same.

This is worth keeping an eye on for a number of different reasons, the most relevant of which is the fact that the Bitcoin blockchain has already reached the peak of its usage capacity. At this point, the Bitcoin blockchain can only process about seven transactions a second which means, at any given time, there are at least three million transactions that have been verified and are just waiting to be approved by the blockchain itself. As such, even if new transactions stopped being recorded today, it would take the blockchain five full days to catch up. The simple truth is that the basis of the Bitcoin blockchain is code that is nearly a decade old and it can't keep up with its current level of demand.

This fact, coupled with the improved ease of use of smart contracts on its platform, have led many of the leading developers in the blockchain space to switch their apps over to the Ethereum blockchain instead. Ethereum is optimized for a much higher number of transactions per second, and the fees for each of these transactions is lower as well. What it all boils down to is that experts are already predicting that Ethereum will see as much as a ten-fold increase in popularity before the end of 2017.

Also of note is the fact that many of the applications currently under development are being developed with the focus of making the cryptocurrency process more accessible to common users and easier to understand overall. As these projects begin to come online in the next few years it is likely that they will cause usage rates to increase even more. This, in turn, makes it a strong contender to survive past the saturation point and cause its price to increase dramatically. Even more encouraging is the fact that major corporations including JPMorgan and Microsoft have already thrown their lot in with Ethereum by joining the Enterprise Ethereum Alliance.

Finally, the Ethereum platform is still growing and evolving with new upgrades coming down the pipeline on a regular basis. These include upcoming scalability improvements which means it will be able to handle more than one million transactions a second by the end of 2017. This number is currently sitting at fourteen transactions per second so the increase is going to be quite significant. The upcoming switch to a proof of stake model is also due to cut down on the risk of miner centralization, 51 percent attacks and combat inflation. While there will be more than one winner once cryptocurrencies reach the saturation point, Ethereum's infrastructure improvements likely mean that it will be a horse worth backing in the coming years.

CHAPTER 5: MINING CRYPTOCURRENCY

While Bitcoin, once again, holds a monopoly on the current mindshare when it comes to mining, it is far from the only currency that utilizes outside help to verify its transactions. In fact, every cryptocurrency that uses a proof-of-work model uses a variation of the same process. The mining processed is accomplished through the use of high-powered machines that generally utilize a SHA-256 double round hash process for verification purposes in order to ensure the security and sanctity of the blockchain in question. The speed at which a given machine can validate transactions is measured in hashes per second.

In exchange for your work, you will receive an amount of the currency in question that will offset your costs along with making it somewhat worth your while. Additionally, many cryptocurrencies have a transaction fee that goes to the person who mines the block that the transaction is included in as well. The greater the processing power of your mining machine, the greater your odds of completing a block and the more you will make as a result.

The most common type of proof-of-work is what is known as the hashcash proof-of-work and it is a type of cryptographic algorithm which makes use of a hash function as a core part of the process. Hashcash proofs can be tweaked for difficulty in order to ensure that new blocks are not generated at a faster rate than the network can handle which means block generation is tied to the number of transactions that can be processed per second. For example, a new blockchain block cannot be created more than once every ten minutes. The probability of a successful generation is relatively low which means it is nearly impossible to determine which mining machine is going to generate the next block.

In order for a new block to be seen as valid, its hash value must ultimately end up being less than that of the current target which means that each block then naturally shows the work that has been done to generate it. Each block also contains the hash of the block that precedes it which is how the chain is able to determine where in the chain it belongs. This means that a block can only be changed if the work done to all the previous blocks is also redone and new hashes are created for each of them in order.

Starting mining

What constitutes the best mining hardware and the best prices for it are always in flux which means you are going to need to do some external research before you get started. You can find a breakdown of the state of the art hardware that is currently being used on the Bitcoin reddit and many of the latest and greatest mining machines can be found on Amazon.com or with a simple Google search.

Regardless of the system you go with, you are going to need dedicated hardware to do so effectively. While you could theoretically mine using your standard computer or laptop's CPU or video card, specialized machines are built for speed with this specific task in mind which means those running them would steal any blocks you were assigned out from under you before you could even hope to finish the required calculations.

Customized chips made by the ASIC company dominate the market in the summer of 2017 and typically offer speeds as much as 100 times that of what the average PC can provide. Trying to mine without this specialized hardware will generally just end up costing you more in fees for electricity than you will ever earn as a result. Specialized Bitcoin mining machines typically sell from anywhere from $500 to $3,500.

Download the software: After you have purchased a mining machine, the next thing that you are going to need to do is download the program that is used in the mining process. There are several different versions of this software on the market today, though the most used ones are BFGminer and CGminer which run via command line commands. If you are looking for something easier and with a graphical interface, then EasyMiner utilizes a more modern interface and is available for all major hardware platforms.

Join a mining pool: After you have the hardware and the software in place, the next thing you are going to want to do is joining a mining pool for your chosen cryptocurrency. A mining pool is a loose affiliation of miners who join together for the purpose of verifying blocks as quickly as possible. The rewards for doing so are then shared amongst all of the miners who contributed computational power to the process. While joining a mining pool is optional, it is recommended as the number of blocks you will be a part of mining will be much higher than it would otherwise be if you decided to go it alone.

This is due to the fact that the amount of computational power required to generate an accurate proof of work for most blockchains in a reasonable period of time is on the rise which means mining pools have quickly become the new norm for nearly all blockchains that see serious use. Those who contribute to solving a proof the receive a share of the profits based on one of several different compensation models.

If you decide to go it alone then you will need to download what is known as the core client to keep your machine in sync with the blockchain as a whole. This client can be downloaded from the cryptocurrency in question's primary website. Assuming you do choose to participate in a mining pool, all you will need to do is follow the instructions of the pool manager and make sure to always engage in behavior that is in agreement with the terms of use of the blockchain in question.

Choosing the right mining pool for you can be quite a complicated process, simply because there are so many active ones to choose from. The best way to see what options are available for your cryptocurrency of choice is going to be by searching for it on Reddit. This will also let you read comments about each so that you don't sign up with a lemon. While joining up with one of the most popular pools means you will be in the running for more potential verifications, it also means that you will receive a smaller share of the compensation that you will receive for your work. Additionally, the overall hashrate distribution is always going to remain higher when split among a larger overall selection of mining pools. It is generally considered better for the health of the blockchain if you choose a mining pool that is somewhat smaller, though still large enough to ensure that a steady string of proofs is generated on a regular basis.

Making a profit: Assuming you sign up with a mining pool, determining your share of the profits is also going to be a complicated process. There are a wide variety of different ways that compensation is calculated which means you are going to want to be familiar with the most popular ones before you choose a mining pool to sign up with to ensure you know what you are really getting into.

The pay per share (PPS) model of compensation pays out miners as soon as the block has been mined with a set amount for each share of the proof that is solved by that miner's machine. Miners are paid out from the balance that the pool current holds which means they can take their share of the profits without waiting for the transaction to be verified by the chain and payment to be transferred. This is the payment structure that allows for the least amount of variance in what miners can expect to receive and it leaves the brunt of the risk on the pool operator should anyone not go according to plan.

As there are always risks that a payout might not go through as anticipated, even when a proof is created successfully, PPS payments require the operator to have a large reserve of the cryptocurrency in question in order to remain solvent during prolonged periods of bad luck. As such, the PPS model is not especially common anymore among most of the more popular types of cryptocurrency.

The proportional approach to mining offers a distribution of the rewards for mining a block in a proportional amount so that each miner receives an amount in proportion to the portion of the proof that they provided. Payments are then generated once the block has been accepted by the blockchain and payment has been delivered.

The pay per last N share (PPLN) payment method is generally similar to the proportional method except it works based on N shares instead of traditional shares. The main difference between this and the PPS method which offers a set rate for each share is that N shares pay out based on the amount that is generated per block which means the amount each miner will be paid varies as well. Payments are then generated after they have been paid out by the blockchain.

The double geometric payment method (DGM) is a hybrid approach that ensures any inherent risk is split between the pool manager and the miners. The manager receives a portion of the profits when the pool is mining a lot of blocks and then returns a portion of that to the miners when things are slow or the work the pool is doing is extremely complex. The payments are then based on shares and are paid out once the block has been accepted to the blockchain.

The shared maximum pay per share model (SMPPS) is a variation of the pay per share model that is used more frequently these days. It offers a set amount per share that fluctuates based on the amount of rewards the pool has earned over a set period of time. Payments are made once the time period has elapsed and the blocks have been accepted by the chain.

The recently shared maximum pay per share model (RSMPPS) is similar to SMPPS but it prioritizes the newest members of the pool so that new miners are more likely to get shares than those that have been in the pool the longest. Payments are made on a set schedule once the blocks have been verified and accepted into the chain.

The capped pay per share with recent back pay (CPPSRB) model works via a variation of the MPPS model and pays out miners to the maximum degree possible based on the blocks it gains access to while also ensuring that the pool never goes bankrupt as a result. Payments are made after the blocks have been verified and accepted.

The pooled mining model (PMM) is also known as the slush pool, is a method of payment whereby later shares of a given block are given a higher percentage when compared to earlier shares as they often require more resources to mine effectively. This method also has the benefit of making it difficult for miners to switch horses midstream in an effort to maximize their personal profits. Payments are made after the block has been mined successfully and accepted into the chain.

The pay on target (POT) model of payment is another variation on the standard PPS model that pays out its miners based on the amount of resources each used in order to help mine the block successfully. Payments are made after the round has finished and the block has been verified by the blockchain.

The SCORE model of payment is an approach that utilizes a reward system that is proportionally weighed and distributed based on the amount of time that elapses based on when a block was taken and when it was finished. It also pays out a weighted amount to later shares of the proof to compensate for their added difficulty. Payments are then calculated based on scores given to each miner, not based on shares. Payments are made after the round has finished and the block has been accepted to the blockchain.

The eligius payment model was created by the person who created BFGMiner and looks to take the strengths of the PPS model along with those of the BPM model. It generates shares for miners that can be paid out as soon as the work is completed. Once the rewards for the block come in, they are then divided equally amongst all the shares that went into the block with stale blocks (those that could not be completed) having their shares rolled over into the shares of the next successfully completed block. Payments are only sent through once a miner earns at least .67108864 of the shares of a given block with lesser amounts being paid out once the miner doesn't mine anything for seven days. If a miner doesn't have enough shares then their shares are rolled over into the next block as well.

The triple mining payment method puts together multiple smaller pools with no extra fees and then gives each miner one percent of each block to mine. This typically results in miners who receive larger shares overall when compared to other types of payment methods. The managers who run this process with then take a portion of the profits from each block to add to a jackpot that the miner who originally found the block is awarded.

This means that everyone in the grouped together pools then has a proportionally greater chance to make an additional profit regardless of the processing power that they bring to the table.

CHAPTER 6: AVOIDING FRAUD

Due to the fact that the cryptocurrency market is extremely unregulated, and the amount of money floating around in it currently, scammers are trying every conceivable method possible to make money off of those who are ignorant to the risks they face. This chapter outlines a wide variety of ways that scammers are trying to take advantage of the cryptocurrency market today, but it is important to keep in mind that they are always looking for new ways to get one over on you which means it is important that you never do business with any company that isn't reputable in order to ensure that your money stays safely where it belongs.

Fake exchanges: While some cryptocurrency exchanges are less reputable than others, most at least try to provide a legitimate service to consumers. This is not the case with exchanges at the bottom of the barrel, however, as they are typically fake from the start and are simply looking to take money from the uninformed and vanish into the ether with it. The easiest way to determine if an exchange is a scam or not is based on its advertisements. If the exchange is offering to sell you a cryptocurrency at a flat rate that is below its current market value then the is a ninety-five percent chance that they are only looking to take your money. Cryptocurrency exchanges work in the same way that any other exchange does which is to say that users buy and sell currency to one another. As no user is going to expect less than market value for their cryptocurrency, this is a red flag that something fishy is going on.

The other red flag you should be aware of is if you come across an exchange that is offering to buy your cryptocurrency directly through PayPal. This is also not how exchanges work. If you buy into a particular exchange using your cryptocurrency then that cryptocurrency doesn't leave your possession until someone else has paid for it through legitimate channels. These types of scams have you enter your PayPal details and then tell you to send your cryptocurrency to another address, typically found on a QR code so it is especially easy for them to change it when the jig is up. Of course, once you send off your Bitcoins the promised payment will never materialize and you will not be able to get in contact with the exchange directly. In general, it is never a good idea to sell your cryptocurrency outside the boundaries of a reputable exchange.

Fake wallets: Spotting a fake cryptocurrency wallet can be more difficult than spotting a fake exchange simply due to the fact that they store your cryptocurrency as opposed to buying and selling it which means the fraudulent part is generally going to come in the form of malicious software that will attack your phone or computer in an effort to steal your personal data. Officially sanctioned wallets can typically be found on the primary website for the cryptocurrency in question.

The easiest way to determine if a given wallet is fake or not is to listen to your instincts and consider if anything about the website seems off. Additionally, you are going to want to avoid websites whose URL does not include HTTPS at the start as this means it is not secured which means you wouldn't want to enter your personal detail anyway. Before downloading the wallet of your choice, you are going to want to ensure that you entered the URL correctly as similar, but misspelled URLs often lead to fraudulent sites.

Furthermore, if the wallet you are planning on using isn't online and is instead a file that you download you are going to want to ensure that you scan it for known malware before you install it to your hard drive. If you don't have virus software on your computer, you can use the site VirusTotal.com to check it for you. Finally, it is always recommended that you choose a wallet that the cryptocurrency community that you now belong to approves of to see if other people have had success when using the wallet you are thinking about storing your hard-earned cryptocurrency in.

Phishing scams: Another scam that you are likely to see a lot of is the cryptocurrency phishing scam. This scam involves the scammer trying to trick you into thinking they are an authority from either the website for the cryptocurrency you are using or from the exchange you are a part of. They will generally tend to recommend that you visit some website which will then proceed to ruin your day. The most common version of this scam involves sending you an email requesting your presence, though popup advertisements may work the same way. Either way, the end result is either going to infect your computer with malware or end with the scammer trying to steal your cryptocurrency directly.

If you receive an email that doesn't seem entirely on the level, the first thing you are going to want to do is to never take the bait. This can be easier said than done, however, as the email may very well appear legitimate either because the exchange you use has had their database hacked or because the scammer has gotten ahold of your email address via other nefarious means.

Regardless, the best practice is going to involve never opening any proffered attachments or clicking on hyperlinks in emails whose sender you cannot verify. If you have legitimate business with the website in question, instead of responding to that email, visit the site directly and look for contact details before asking a real person about it. Another common tactic that scammers use is to create an official looking hyperlink but this can be countered by looking at the URL it is sending you to by simply holding your cursor over it and looking at the web address that pops up.

Finally, you will always want to verify the address of the person who sent the email. While it is possible that the address is fake or was spoofed, this will often give you an idea of whether or not it is on the level. More than anything else, knowing that these scams are out there should make it much easier to avoid them.

When it comes to dealing with fake online advertisements, it is important that you are careful about the sites you go to online. The most common way that unsuspecting users get pulled into these types of phishing scams is by doing an online search for something related to cryptocurrency and then clicking on the first link that comes up without even really looking at it. This is a poor choice, however, as this first link is almost always going to be sponsored content and just as frequently lead to a scam of one type or another. You can avoid this risk completely by simply knowing where you are going online and entering the URL in question directly.

Ponzi scams: The exact specifics of a cryptocurrency Ponzi scam might vary, but they all have one thing in common, they require that you send in your cryptocurrency in exchange for a better than average return on your investment. The most common version of this type of scam claims that it can double the amount of cryptocurrency that you provide them within a short amount of time. They are also easy to spot due to the fact that they typically work on a referral system that encourages those who are already part of the program to get those whom they know to sign up as well. If you come across a site that is offering you a commission to get other users to take part in the program, or if you came across the recommendation in an online forum then there is a good chance the program is part of a Ponzi scam. If you are unsure of the validity of a given program, the best place to stay up to date on what is legitimate and what is not is the Reddit page for the cryptocurrency in question.

Mining pools: This is one of the more difficult types of scams to suss out, simply because it will likely appear on the level, at least at first. Odds are, when you first sign up with the fake mining pool, you will receive payments as if you were actually validating blocks, though you will likely be asked to pay a fee to become a part of the pool. The money you make from the pool is actually going to be a portion of the fees that have been collected by other miners which means it is likely to decrease over time as word about what the mining pool really is leaked out to the community.

As always, you are going to want to start by trusting your instincts and checking out the relevant forums in order to determine if anyone else has previously had trouble with the mining pool. If the pool is new then it might not have much of a presence on these sites, but it will be a good way to weed out those that have already been identified as scams. Additionally, when it comes to signing up for a mining pool it is always important to track down the one you are going to use yourself and to never follow any referral links as these will rarely lead to reputable options.

When looking into these services, you will need to keep an eye out for a handful of different details that legitimate pools will provide. This includes things like the pool that they mine from and the ability to choose the pool you wish to contribute your hash rate too. You will also want to be aware of the limits that are expressed in terms of the maximum hashrate that the mining pool can handle, as very few legitimate pools have access to anything close to an unlimited amount due to the fact that hardware of this type is expensive and it takes time to both deploy and acquire. Fake services will not have any limitations in this area, often because they are doing any actual mining in the first place.

While this type of scam might seem relatively benign if you are still making a profit, it is important to keep in mind that unlike with a legitimate service, these payments are going to decrease over time, if they come in at all. Along these lines, it is also easy to determine if a mining pool is a scam if their site starts to cut the rates required to buy into the program. Scammers will typically continue cutting the required rates as low as they need to in order to keep attracting new marks. This process will continue until no one is left who will bite at which point they will take the money they made and the mining operation will fold. Due to the fact that once you buy in they have your money, these types of scams can often go on for months, if not years, as long as the mining pool keeps attracting interest.

You will also want to keep an eye out for mining pools that have an endorsement from a registered ASIC vendor. These vendors provide a large majority of all of the mining machines used by mining pools and, nine out of ten, will provide the pools whose machines they have provided with a certification logo or a post lending credence to the operation. There is no downside for them when it comes to this type of thing as it is a free advertisement while also improving consumer confidence in their brand. If you are thinking about a mining pool that can't provide this information, think twice.

Along similar lines, the mining pool should be able to readily provide pictures of their hardware and data center, and if this information isn't on their website directly then they should be able to provide it to you by request. Regardless of what they say in response, this is a request that only shows you are being careful with your money. If you receive anything but the requested pictures then you will know the operation is a scam.

CHAPTER 7: THE FUTURE OF CRYPTOCURRENCY

The cryptocurrency market is in the midst of a boom phase that has the market in an extreme state of fluctuation as there are so many different cryptocurrencies competing for dominance despite the fact that only a small handful of these are seeing any real type of adoption rate. This fierce competition makes it difficult to determine what the future holds with any significant rate of certainty. However, there are some things that can be intuited by experts based on trends that are currently emerging.

Increasing scrutiny

When it first appeared in 2009, Bitcoin's main benefit was the fact that it was completely decentralized which meant all of its transactions took place anonymously. Those in the know instantly started taking advantage of this fact in order to do all manner of illegal things on the darknet, primarily via the Silk Road marketplace. Now that cryptocurrency is starting to become more mainstream. Governmental and regulatory agencies around the world, including the Securities and Exchange Commission, the Federal Bureau of Investigations, the Department of Homeland Security and the Financial Crimes Enforcement Network, in the US, alone are all giving it much more attention.

This increasing level of scrutiny began ramping up in 2013 when the Financial Crimes Enforcement Network first begin issuing rulings that declared cryptocurrency exchanges were actually money service businesses which meant they had to follow government regulations. The Department of Homeland Security soon followed up on this ruling by freezing the accounts of the biggest Bitcoin exchange the world had seen at that time, called Mt. Gox, most of which were held by Wells Fargo, due to concerns related to money laundering.

This directly lead to an April 2017 ruling by the Securities and Exchange Commission to deny an application by Bitcoin to open an official cryptocurrency exchange trade fund, a move that caused a noticeable decrease in the cryptocurrency's price, though not for long. This denial of the application is currently under review in the summer of 2017.

This has left cryptocurrency in a bit of an odd situation as their increasing popularity has led them to additional levels of governmental scrutiny and required regulation which directly goes against the reasons they were created in the first place. Additionally, while the number of regular users is growing every day, it is still a small portion of the numbers that will ultimately be needed in order for cryptocurrency to reach a mass saturation point. If these issues have not been solved by the time this level of acceptance is reached, it is unlikely that they ever will.

In order for a cryptocurrency to reach a true level of mainstream status and become a true part of the incumbent financial system, it is going to need to be able to stay true to its original purpose and also remain complex enough that its overall level of security remains at or above the current level of security protocols. On the other hand, it would need to become easy enough for the average person to truly understand. It would also need to be decentralized enough that it can still be recognized as adjacent to its original form while still having checks in place to ensure that unsavory activities like tax evasion and money laundering can't proceed unchecked. This means that the cryptocurrencies of the future might be more an amalgamation of its current form and the more traditional types of fiat currencies.

Governmental oversight

US: While the United States is currently actively looking into way to ensure that Bitcoins aren't being used as a means to launder money nor as a way to fund illegal activity, analysts who are in the know also say that the federal government is currently working out plans for issuing its own form of cryptocurrency as well to more effectively cut

 the problems off at the source and not have to deal with wrangling an uncooperative technology in the first place. This idea, which is being referred to unofficially as Fedcoin, posits that the Federal Reserve, as a national bank, could create a unique type of cryptocurrency with relative ease. All that it would have to do is to create its own blockchain and then generate the required genesis block. FEDcoins could then be easily exchanged for actual dollars at a rate of 1 to 1, at least at first.

The only real difference between Fedcoin and other cryptocurrencies currently in existence would be in the fact that a single user, namely the federal government, would then be able to create new blocks at will or destroy those that it had reason to believe were being used to finance illegal activities. This could be done by simply forking the protocol of Bitcoin, or more likely Ethereum, and then adjust the reward for mining blocks based on its own needs. This would lead to a type of cryptocurrency that would be both decentralized when it came to the individual transaction and centralized when it came to limiting supply and monitoring those previously anonymous transactions.

While this might seem like something of a conspiracy theory, the fact of the matter is that the authorities of the Federal Reserve met with Bitcoin authorities in a closed-door meeting in the fall of 2016. Janet Yellen, the Chair of the Federal Reserve oversaw the conference herself which also included banking heavyweights from the World Bank, the Bank for International Settlements, the International Monetary fund and more.

Officially the focus of the meeting was on utilizing blockchain as a means of improving the efficacy of intra-banking transfers but insiders say that issuing a federal cryptocurrency was also a topic that was discussed at length. The CEO of the company Chain, a blockchain based company even delivered a speech with the title "Why Central

Banks Will Issue Digital Currencies" during which he urged governments to take control of cryptocurrencies themselves.

One of the most pressing arguments for Fedcoin seems to be the Federal Reserve's desire to stabilize cryptocurrency as a whole by connecting it directly to physical money. This link would not need to be voluntary either as the new Fedcoin would likely be optional at first but eventually, it would be harder and harder to find physical money in use anywhere.

Russia: Russia experienced a serious change of heart when it comes to cryptocurrencies in 2017. They announced that cryptocurrency use was legalized after a statement in 2016 indicated that those who used the digital currency could face jail time. The reason behind this abrupt 180 seems to stem from Russia's currently ongoing problem with corruption in its banking sector. Since 2014, the Russian economy has been under extreme strain due to a decrease in oil prices combined with foreign sanctions that have extremely curtailed foreign investment. This, in turn, has led to heightened costs when it comes to accessing money which has led to a decline in the banking sector.

This downturn has come during a serious push by the Russian Central Bank to combat corruption at all levels amidst fears that many banks have been removing capital from the country via complex money-laundering schemes. As of summer 2017, more than one hundred banks have been closed in the past three years with nearly that many being expected to close by 2019. This has been a serious financial drain on the country to the tune of more than $50 billion so far. This process has also brought to light concerns about liquidity for the country as a whole and the feeling among analysts is that the Central Bank needs to tread carefully or risk, provoking a crisis of epic magnitude; thus, the change in cryptocurrency policy.

As an added bonus, an increased focus on digital currencies would decrease the importance of the interpersonal relationship between region administrators, local businesses, and banks which will ideally decrease corruption levels as well. The current system of credit in Russia is practically opaque to the point that Central Bank authorities often don't even know who is involved in the regional banking system and smaller banks are essentially autonomous.

This problem apparently hasn't been solved by the bank closing spree and fraud is still rampant which is why the Russian government has been experimenting with a variety of technical applications designed to make it easier for them to identify transactions in real time. The use of a variation of the Fedcoin is not what the national government is currently interested in, however, and they currently have their attention focused on blockchain technology in general. Specifically, there are interested in the ease with which it allows individual transactions to be tracked.

It is currently unclear if Russia is planning to adapt the existing Bitcoin blockchain for its own ends or if it is planning on creating its own via new legislation. On the other hand, it may be planning to make use of the existing platform for a time while allowing its own banks to develop their own system or take a closer look at the system as a means of better understanding how blockchain can help to mitigate their financial woes. It is also currently unclear if the leadership in Moscow is going to support or fight against these changes, though the announced change in cryptocurrency policy gives strong indications of the former as opposed to the later.

China: Once again, China proves that it is at the forefront of the cryptocurrency revolution as they announced in June of 2017 that the People's Bank of China created the first prototype of its own digital currency that has the ability to scale seamlessly based on the number of transactions that take place in a day. While the exact details are not clear, speeches and research papers that have been released on the topic apparently indicate that the bank is planning to release the cryptocurrency to the public at the same time as the renminbi, though no official timetable is available for when exactly that might be. Despite the lack of a firm rollout date, the cryptocurrency has already been tested via transactions between the People's Bank and several of the country's leading commercial banks.

This testing is a significant step for the idea of officially sanctioned cryptocurrencies and shows that China is extremely committed to exploring the logistical, technical and economic challenges involved in developing its own digital currency which is sure to have far-reaching implications for the global financial system and its economy in particular. This is due to the fact that a digital fiat currency, a cryptocurrency that is backed by a central bank and essentially has the same status as a banknote, would serve to dramatically lower the transactions costs associated with all financial transactions which would go a long way towards making financial services more widely available to the parts of the world that do not currently have access to these services. It would also mark a significant step forward for China as a whole as there are millions there who still lack the types of banking services that those many countries take for granted.

Perhaps more important to the Chinese government than improving its people's access to these services is the fact that a centralized cryptocurrency would give them more control over the types of digital transaction that have become extremely popular in China over the past few years. Additionally, a centralized digital currency would be easier to track which would make it easier for the government to crackdown on corruption as well.

Also of interest to policymakers, this type of digital system would make it easier to offer real-time insight into the local economy which could benefit the country as a whole as well. It will also make it easier to expand the reach of the renminbi as intra-country transactions would be much easier to complete as well and the currency would be easier to obtain than it is via current methods.

Other countries are also going to be interested in the results of China's cryptocurrency project as it is said to integrate smoothly with the central banking system. The new cryptocurrency is said to provide cryptocurrency wallets to the central banking branches which would make it easy for anyone to set up a digital account that uses the new cryptocurrency.

Also of interest is the fact that the cryptocurrency is said to not be based on the traditional blockchain architecture that powers virtually every cryptocurrency on the market today. Rather, it makes use of a limited distributed ledger systems as a means of getting around the potential for bottlenecks that are inherent in many blockchains. Instead, it only accesses the digital ledger to occasionally update its records and determine who holds what and how long they have been holding it.

CONCLUSION

Thank you for making it through to the end of *Cryptocurrency: How to Make a Lot of Money Investing and Trading in Cryptocurrency*, let's hope it was informative and able to provide you with all of the tools you need to achieve your goals, whatever it is that they may be. Just because you've finished this book doesn't mean there is nothing left to learn on the topic, expanding your horizons is the only way to find the mastery you seek.

As you have no doubt realized, cryptocurrency is still in a state of extreme fluctuation which means that the only way to truly stay on the forefront of what is happening in the market is to make lifelong learning a habit. If you instead decide to rest on your laurels you never know when you might miss out on a crucial news or the next big thing. Eventually, things will settle down into a relatively stable status quo, but that won't happen anytime soon.

The next thing you are going to want to do is to stop reading already and to get ready to get started making money from this unprecedented time in the history of currency. Never again in your lifetime will you see so many different currencies competing for dominance in a market that will ultimately be able to only support a few of them. This means that in order to make the right decisions to prevent yourself from backing the wrong horse you are going to need to do your homework and never make a move without fully considering all your options.

It is also important to keep in mind that, even more so than other types of investing, investing in cryptocurrency is far from a sure thing. This is a fact you are going to have to come to terms with, as it is equally likely that you will lose your investment as it is that you will make the type of choice that leads to a serious payout in the future. Overall, it is key that you remember that a serious windfall is unlikely to fall into your lap anytime soon and that investing in cryptocurrency is a marathon, not a sprint, slow and steady wins the race.

Finally, if you found this book useful in any way, a review on Amazon is always appreciated!

Made in the USA
San Bernardino, CA
12 December 2017